WILES on the WATER

A light-hearted look at fly-fishing for trout

FISHING

"We'll see who's got the cunning and guile before the season's out!"

WILES on the WATER

A light-hearted look at fly-fishing for trout
By

Arnold WILES.

TROUT & SALMON

LITTLE, BROWN AND COMPANY

A *Little, Brown* Book

First published in Great Britain in 1994 by
Little, Brown and Company

A CIP catalogue record for this book is
available from the British Library.

ISBN 0 316 91118 6

Typeset by M Rules
Printed and bound in Great Britain by
BPC Hazell Books Ltd

Little, Brown and Company (UK) Limited
Brettenham House
Lancaster Place
London WC2E 7EN

FLY-FISHING & FLY-TYING

FOREWORD

Sometimes it's hard to imagine how fly-fishing ever caught on as a popular pastime. Every angler, at some stage of their fly-fishing career, must have wondered who it was that first had the absurd notion to entice a trout into taking a hook disguised with pieces of fur and feather – usually after a third 'blank' in a row. And what of the novice fly-tyer, struggling to learn his craft? Hours at the vice trying to bind small bunches of fur and slips of feather to a hook, often so tiny, it can barely be seen without the aid of a magnifying glass. A skill only brought to some sort of perfection after much frustration; a frustration increased tenfold when the tyer's favourite creation is completely ignored on the water by fish rising all around to the natural insect in a frenzy of feeding. On this evidence, it's not surprising that the uninitiated regard fly-fishermen with a wary and suspicious eye, normally reserved for the clinically insane.

Analyse fly-fishing closely, and you begin to wonder why we take it so seriously; but serious we are, sometimes perhaps a little too much for our own good. Luckily, in Arnold Wiles and the characters he draws we have the medium to defuse such solemnity. Only a fly-fisherman can identify the situations and can have experienced the perplexities, curiosities, dumbfoundedness, incredulousness, horror, exasperation, frustration and embarrassment that are synonymous with the sport. Arnold Wiles has the unique combination of expertise with a cartoonist's pen, a fertile imagination, and, above all, a full grounding in fly-fishing matters, which enable him to portray all these expressions and more on the faces of his characters, in situations we all recognise and (almost always) believe. You see, he's 'been there' and put himself through the fly-fishing mill, just like you and me.

So, as you stand in the lake or on the river bank, flogging your heart out to little or no avail, try to imagine how Arnold Wiles might view your situation. Hopefully, his caricatures and his outlook on the sport will help to remind you that, at the end of the day, fly-fishing is really all about having fun.

Mark Bowler
Editor,
*Fly-fishing and
Fly-tying*

FISHING

WILES on the WATER

A light-hearted look at fly-fishing for trout

THE NEWCOMER TO FLY-FISHING WOULD BE WELL ADVISED TO
INVEST IN PROFESSIONAL CASTING TUITION AT THE OUTSET . . .

TROUT FISHERMAN

"Before we begin, can you read that notice from a distance of thirty metres?"

"I see we are still having trouble with our back cast, Mr Wimple."

"Er, no, Mrs Hatherly, you're not supposed to LASSO them."

THE ABILITY TO CAST LONG DISTANCES MAY OCCASIONALLY BE ADVANTAGEOUS...

"You got out 20 yards of line, all right, but it's supposed to be out there on the water!"

... *BUT ACCURACY IN PLACING THE FLY MAY BE MORE DESIRABLE.*

"It's amazing how their accuracy improves on my specially-trained trout!"

"Yes, it IS a record for the river, and NO my pupils don't usually catch a fish like that with their first cast!"

TROUT FISHERMAN

ATTEMPTING TO TEACH ONESELF
CAN ONLY FOSTER BAD HABITS.

FLY-FISHING FOR BEGINNERS

FISHING

THE STUDY OF AQUATIC AND SOME TERRESTRIAL INSECTS IS INSEPARABLE FROM THE ART OF FLY-FISHING.

TROUT & SALMON

"This is Mr Netwell, my gillie, and Professor Gubbins, my entomologist."

SOME IDEA OF WHAT THE FISH ARE FEEDING ON GREATLY INCREASES ONE'S CHANCE OF CATCHING THEM.

ANGLING TIMES

"I like to know exactly what the trout are feeding on first."

'SPOONING' A TROUT'S STOMACH CONTENTS CAN BE A SHORT-CUT TO
SUCCESS – BUT FIRST YOU MUST CATCH A FISH!

ANGLING TIMES

"Let's ask Sherlock Holmes here what they're feeding on."

NEW-FOUND KNOWLEDGE OF INSECTS LEADS ON FOR MANY TO A DESIRE TO TIE ONE'S OWN FLY IMITATIONS: FURS, FEATHERS AND COLOURED WOOLS IN PROFUSION TAKE ON A NEW SIGNIFICANCE.

"There's not a furred or feathered creature for miles around that feels safe from his depredations when he's tying his flies."

FLY-FISHING & FLY-TYING

"Now that's what I call a HAT!"

FLIES CAN BE TIED IN
ANY ODD CORNER . . .

"They're slashing at some sort of fry over by the dam. I suppose you don't happen to have some yellow fluorescent chenille on you?"

A SPARSE USE OF MATERIALS IS PREFERABLE.

"He tends to overdress his flies as well . . ."

THE OLD 'DRY-FLY ONLY' ETHIC STILL LINGERS IN SOME PURIST HEARTS.

"And remember — Daddy never discusses religion, politics or wet-fly fishing."

"Come, come, sir. You'll surely concede that wet gives way to dry?"

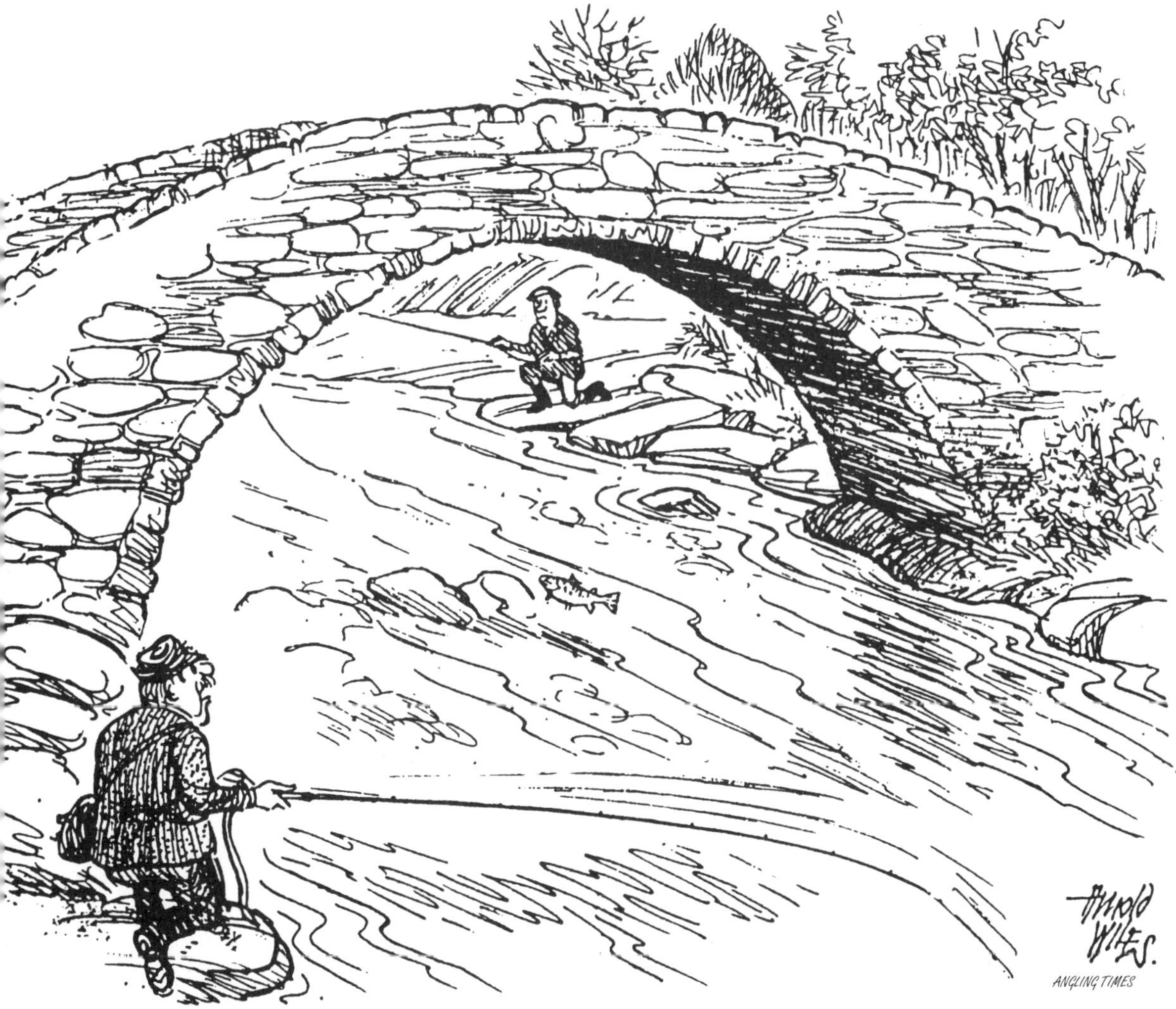
ANGLING TIMES

'DRY-FLY ONLY' FOR THE MORE LIBERAL-MINDED, HAS CONNOTATIONS OF PISCATORIAL SNOBBERY.

"But he MUST be a member. Dammit, if he weren't using a dry-fly, I'd ask to see his credentials."

ON SOME HALLOWED WATERS EVEN THE FISH ARE SUSPECT!

FISHING

"Ruddy snob! You don't see fish like that hovering about in LOWER Niddle water,
now do you?"

SOME FLY PATTERNS ATTEMPT A CLOSE IMITATION OF THE ORIGINAL;
THE BLUE-WINGED OLIVE, (B.W.O.) FOR INSTANCE.

"A B.W.O. often does the trick but today it's been N.B.G. at all."

LURES ARE DESIGNED TO STIMULATE THE TROUT'S AGGRESSIVE INSTINCTS WITH GAUDY COLOURS AND ENTICING MOVEMENT. THE DOG NOBBLER AND THE CAT'S WHISKERS ARE TWO EXAMPLES.

'LURE-STRIPPING', ALTHOUGH MUCH PRACTISED ON STILL WATERS, IS FROWNED UPON BY SOME.

"Don't know what it's called but it certainly catches fish!"

WHATEVER THEIR APPEAL TO FISH OR ANGLER, THEY CERTAINLY
MAKE A COLOURFUL SHOW ON THE BANK!

MANY ANGLERS HAVE A FAVOURITE FLY WHICH THEY WOULD BE LOATH TO PART WITH.

"You're not going to break the barb off? That's my favourite lure!"

WORM-FISHING IS, OF COURSE, UNTHINKABLE.

"It may LOOK like a worm, sir, but I assure you it's made
entirely of feathers!"

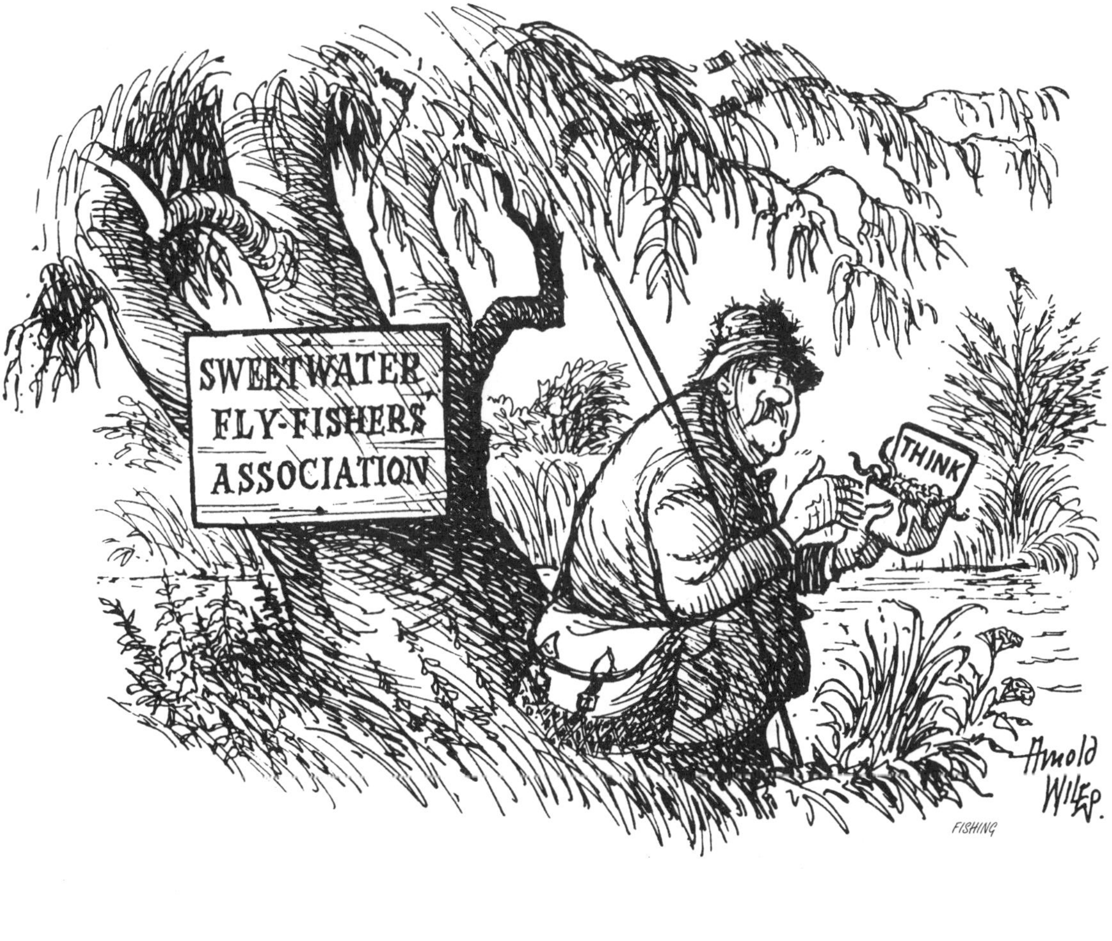
SWEETWATER
FLY-FISHERS
ASSOCIATION
THINK
Arnold Wiles.
FISHING

DRY-FLY, NYMPH AND LURE PATTERNS ARE LEGION; CHOOSING ONE OR THE OTHER CAN BE QUITE A PROBLEM.

"By the time he decides which fly to use, the rise is over."

SOME ANGLERS PUT THEIR FAITH IN JUST A FEW PATTERNS.

"Never use more than three flies, myself . . ."

SOME HAVE AN INSTINCT FOR THE RIGHT FLY . . .

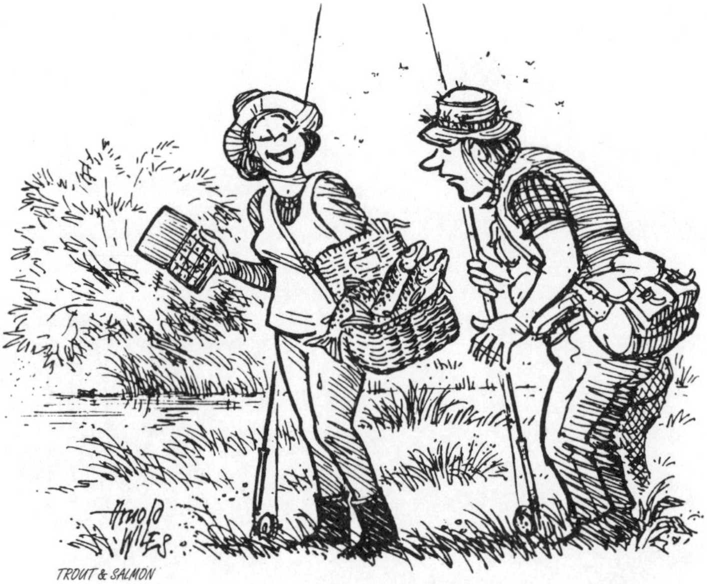
TROUT & SALMON

"I simply chose the prettiest fly in the box."

. . . WHILE OTHERS CHUCK OUT ANY OLD FLY AND HOPE FOR THE BEST.

TROUT FISHERMAN

"I don't know what you want — take your pick, dammit!"

WHETHER TO USE ONE, TWO, OR THREE FLIES ON A CAST IS A MATTER OF PERSONAL PREFERENCE.

ANGLING TIMES

"That's what I call a winning team!"

"Never use more than two flies myself. Imagine what would happen if those were FISH."

TROUT & SALMON

RECOGNISING THE RISE FORM CAN INDICATE THE RIGHT CHOICE OF FLY.

"I've seen bulgers and smutters galore but THAT rise takes the biscuit!"

"What do you think, Fred? Bulging or smutting?"

WHEN CASTING THE DRY-FLY, PRESENTATION IS EVERYTHING. THE IDEA IS TO DECEIVE THE TROUT, NOT SCARE THE LIVING DAYLIGHTS OUT OF THEM.

"Talk about flogging the water. He doesn't hook them — he stuns them!"

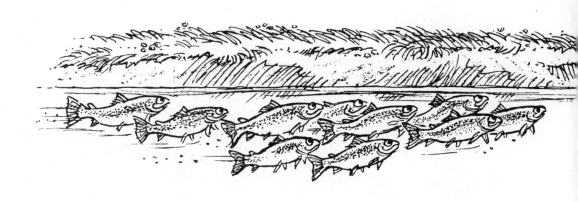

ON SMALL, HARD-FISHED, GIN-CLEAR WATERS, STALKING INDIVIDUAL FISH WITH THE AID OF POLARISED GLASSES FROM BEHIND BANKSIDE COVER, MAY BE THE ORDER OF THE DAY.

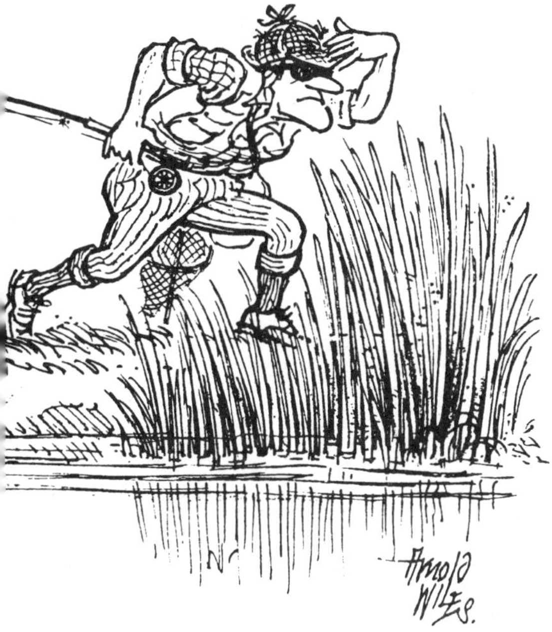

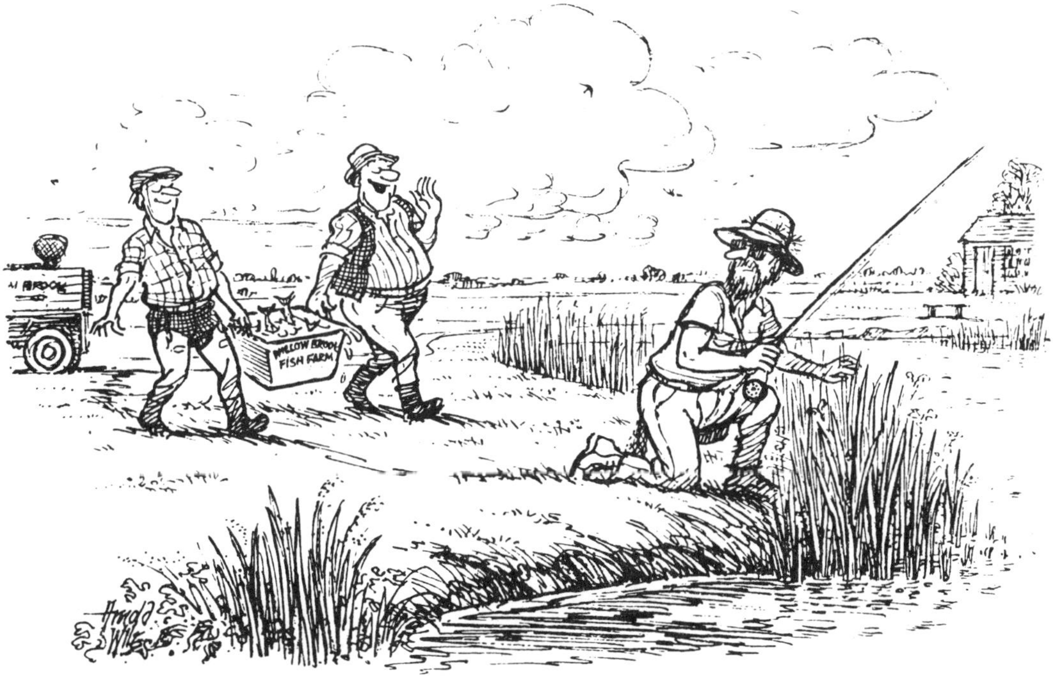
WILLOW BROOK
FISH FARM

"Mind your back!"

THE ANGLING PRESS AND TELEVISION HAVE DONE MUCH TO POPULARISE FLY-FISHING.

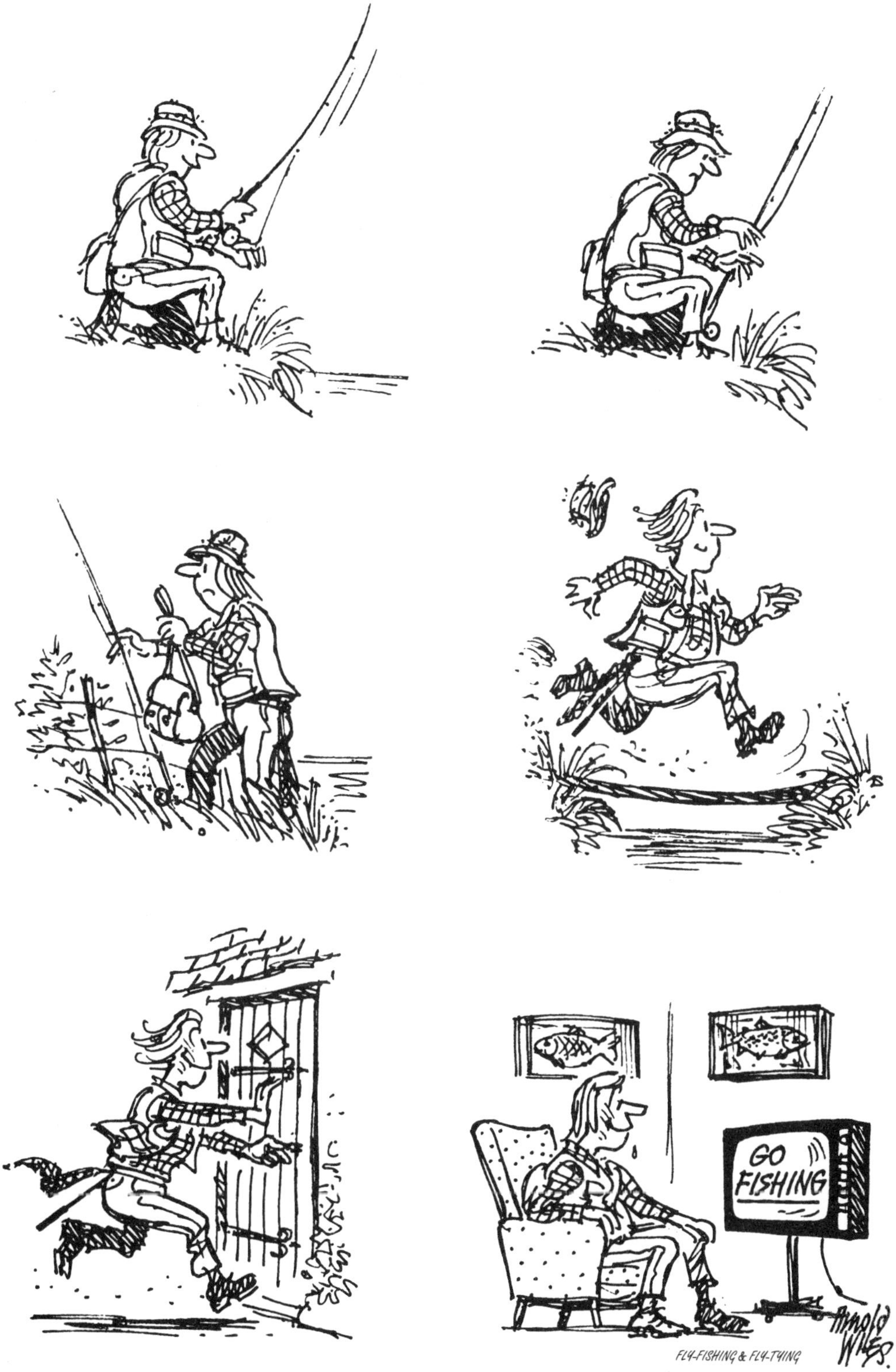
GO FISHING
FLY-FISHING & FLY-TYING
Arnold Wiles.

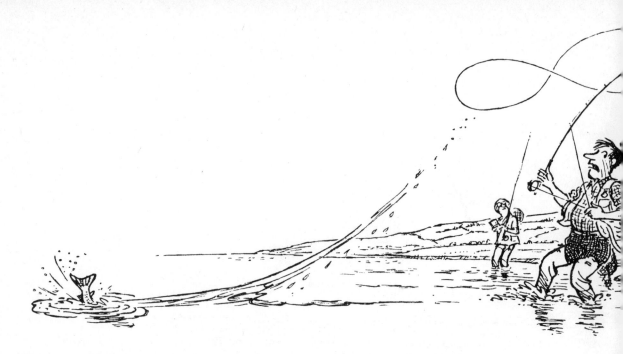

"Damn! The moment I take my eye off the water . . ."

SMALL WONDER THAT WOMEN ARE GRACING THE WATER
IN INCREASING NUMBERS.

THEIR SENSITIVE TOUCH OFTEN
BRINGS A FISH TO NET WHEN THE
MASCULINE APPROACH HAS FAILED.

"Talk about luck! Although it was too cold, the water too low and the fish not in the mood, I managed to catch three."

THE OPENING DAY OF A NEW TROUT-FISHING SEASON IS AWAITED WITH
GREAT ANTICIPATION BY COUNTLESS ANGLERS NATIONWIDE, LEADING
TO A VIRTUAL STAMPEDE ON SOME WATERS.

"Probably some ancient ritual, like Beating the Bounds, to celebrate the opening day."

"It's always the same on opening day — a week from now they'll be complaining that it's fished out!"

MISSING THE OPENING DAY IS UNTHINKABLE FOR SOME . . .

"Haven't missed an opening day in forty years and don't intend to miss one now!"

...AND DRAWING A BLANK A PROSPECT NOT TO BE COUNTENANCED.

"If you say this time last year you had a limit bag, just once more . . ."

"I know night fishing is banned. I'm not putting in a flippin' 'Nil return' on opening day!"

THE WEIGH-IN AT THE END OF THE DAY IS A CEREMONY NOT TO BE MISSED.

TROUT & SALMON

*"Same thing every year! He just can't wait to enter his first fish of the
season in the record book."*

TROUT FISHERMAN

"Any chance of a lift back to the weighing-in hut?"

WITH TODAY'S OVERCROWDED WATERS, SOME FRICTION BETWEEN ANGLERS IS INEVITABLE.

"That's my hat but I'll gladly swop it for your fish!"

"If you drift through my patch just once more . . ."

WADING SHOULD BE AVOIDED; IT SCARES FISH FROM THE BANKS AND DESTROYS WEED AND INSECTS UNDERFOOT.

TROUT & SALMON

"It's handy for getting about, but it does put one at a disadvantage against a low skyline!"

ANGLING TIMES

"What a damn silly place to put a notice board!"

TROUT FISHERMAN

"I know you like to get out among the big ones so I hope all this splashing back here is not disturbing you . . ."

49

EVERY CARE SHOULD BE TAKEN WITH THE BACK-CAST; FLY-FISHERS ARE POTENTIALLY DANGEROUS ANIMALS, NOT ONLY TO ONE ANOTHER.

"That's the trouble with being a doctor — I don't get a chance to wet a line on a reservoir, these days."

"Would you mind running up and down a bit? I haven't hooked a fish all day."

...AND MUCH GOOD FISHING TIME CAN BE WASTED IN EXTRACTING FLIES FROM BANKSIDE TREES AND BUSHES.

TROUT FISHERMAN

"Who says money doesn't grow on trees? I haven't bought a fly in years!"

"I've seen flying fish before but never up in a tree!"

AT LEAST 30 METRES' DISTANCE SHOULD BE MAINTAINED BETWEEN ANGLERS.

TROUT FISHERMAN

"We know these waters are overcrowded but you are standing in my net."

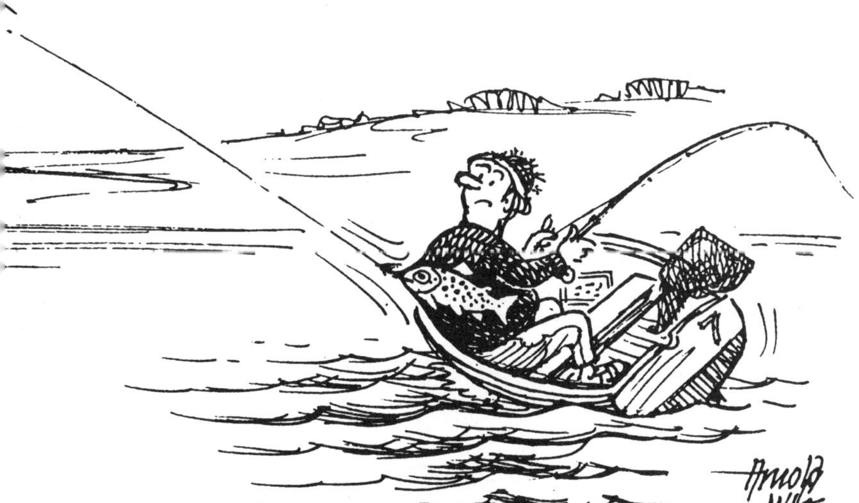
Arnold
Wiles.
ANGLING TIMES

FOR SOME, THE NUMBER OF FISH CAUGHT IN A SEASON
IS ALL IMPORTANT . . .

TROUT FISHERMAN

"With some anglers numbers are EVERYTHING."

. . . BUT BAG LIMITS SHOULD BE
STRICTLY OBSERVED . . .

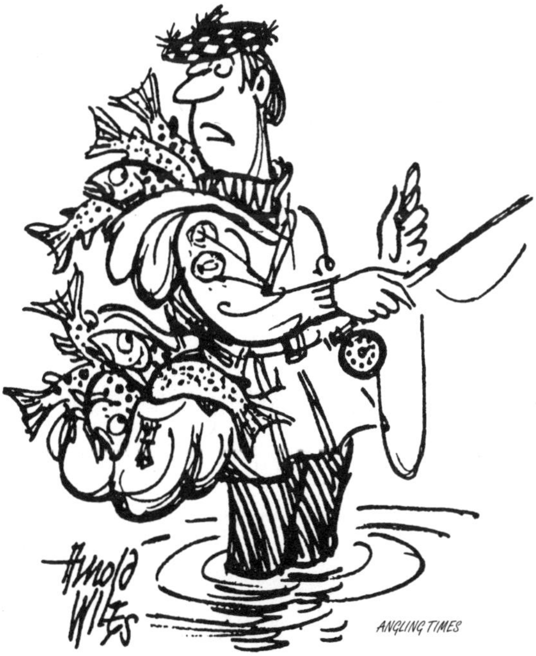
ANGLING TIMES

"Limit bag? What's that?"

...EVEN IF IT PREMATURELY PUTS PAID TO A GOOD DAY OUT.

TROUT FISHERMAN

"Terrible day! Got my limit-bag in the first hour!"

"You know the trouble with this damn lake — it's fished out!"

FOR THE TACKLE PERFECTIONIST, ACTUALLY CATCHING A FISH MAY BE OF SECONDARY IMPORTANCE.

TROUT FISHERMAN

"Never caught a fish. He's got this thing about building the perfect rod."

"As a matter of fact, on my Waller's Mark IV Supafly, carbon-fibre, scientifically tapered rod, with spliced joints and through-the-butt action, coupled with the latest Magiwind reel and high density Magiflow line, I haven't caught a thing all day."

THE *BIG FISH* SYNDROME IS A DISEASE THAT AFFECTS A GOOD MANY.

"It's a woefully long time since I've seen you on your knees in my CHURCH, Colonel Grannom."

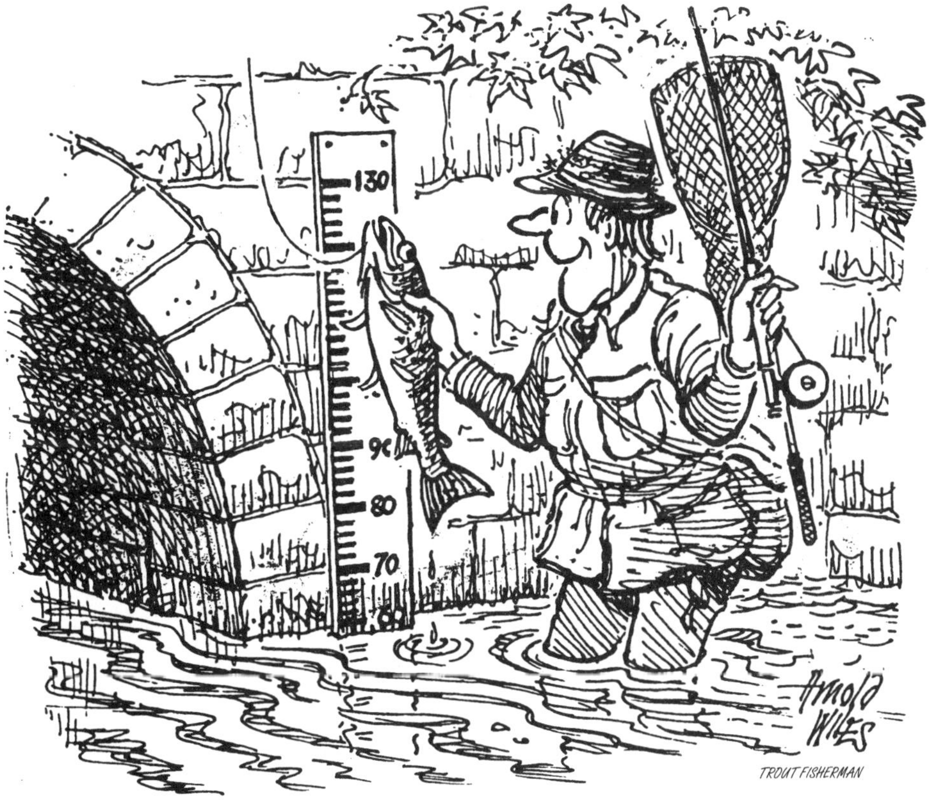
130
90
80
70
Arnold Wiles
TROUT FISHERMAN

"I've a horror of running out of backing."

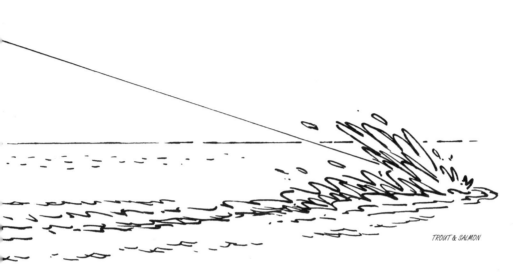

TROUT & SALMON

RUTLAND

ANGLING TIMES

FIGHTING QUALITIES ARE MUCH PRIZED.

ANGLING TIMES

"Talk about fighting qualities — these are acrobatic!"

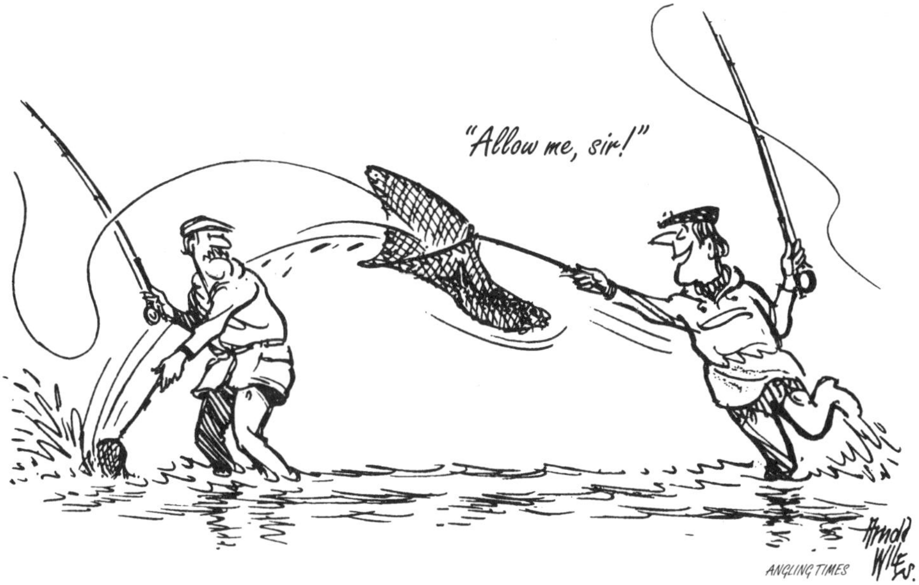
"Allow me, sir!"
ANGLING TIMES

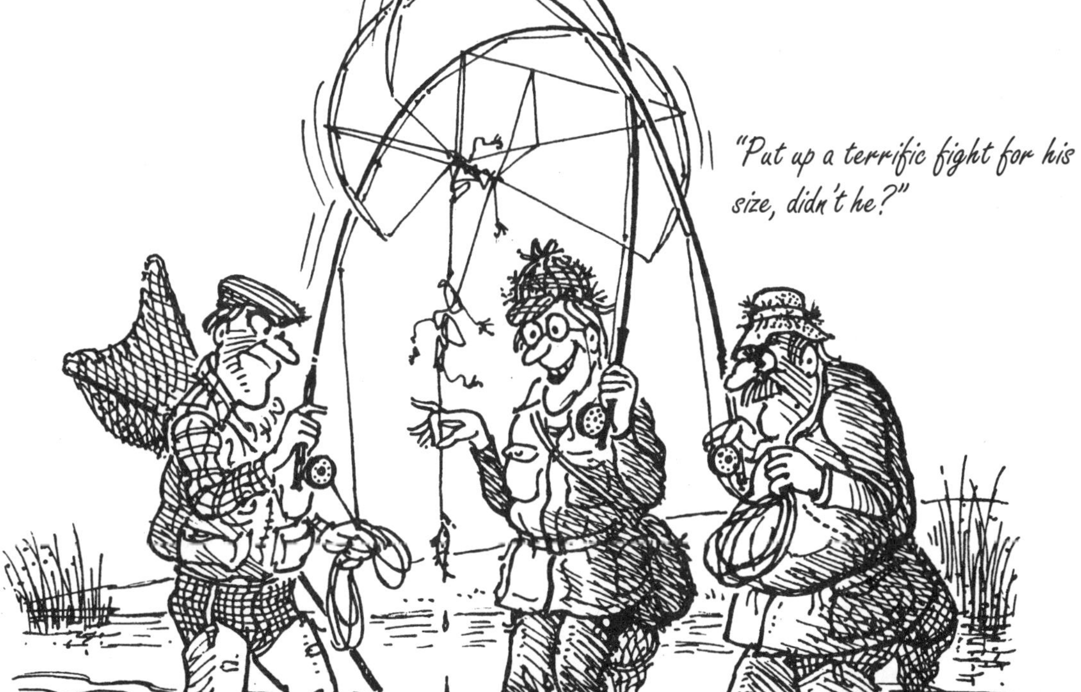
"Put up a terrific fight for his size, didn't he?"

THE DESIRE FOR A 'GLASS CASER' LIES IN MANY AN ANGLER'S BREAST . . .

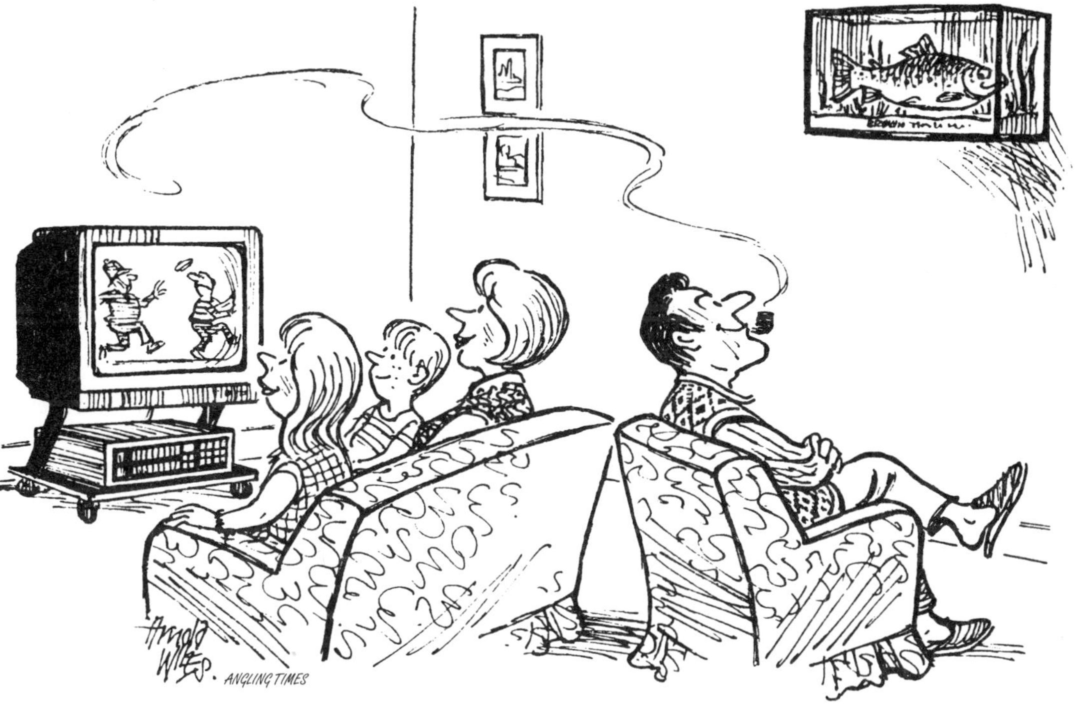
ANGLING TIMES

FISHING

THE COUNTRYMAN

"Just what I want for my husband's birthday! How much a pound are they?"

. . . BUT MOST HAVE TO RELY ON THE CAMERA TO RECORD THE MUCH-PRIZED CATCH.

"It would look much bigger if you removed your sweater, dear."

HOWEVER, REALITY OFTEN FALLS SHORT OF EXPECTATIONS.

"Recognise your special fly? It's in the 'six-pounder' that broke you this morning."

ANGLING TIMES

"Only brought it for the cat? But we haven't GOT a cat!"

FISHING

THERE WILL ALWAYS BE THE BIG — AND NOT SO BIG — FISH THAT GET AWAY.

"Bad luck, vicar! But as the good book says: 'The Lord giveth and the Lord taketh away'."

TROUT & SALMON

"It's HIM! He always waves good-bye."

BLANK DAYS ARE MORE NUMEROUS THAN THE NON-ANGLER MIGHT SUPPOSE...

"That's the only fish we've seen today and he hasn't even got a licence!"

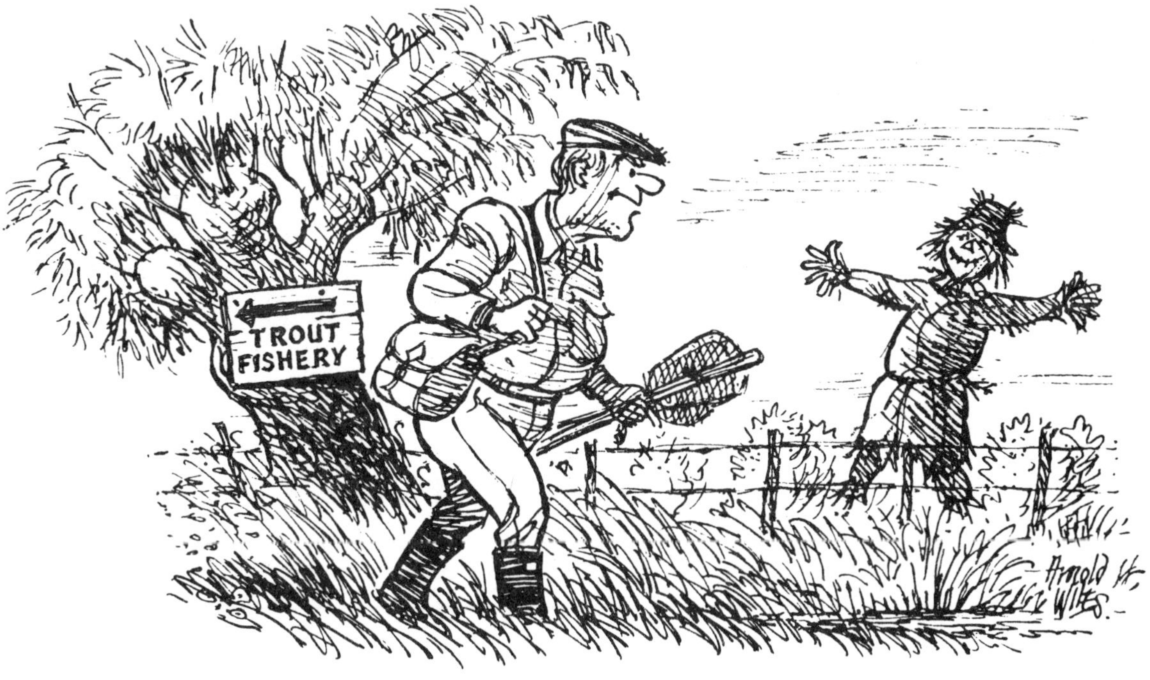
TROUT
FISHERY
Arnold W. Wiles

. . . GIVING RISE TO A RICH FUND OF FACE-SAVING EXCUSES FOR AN EMPTY BAG.

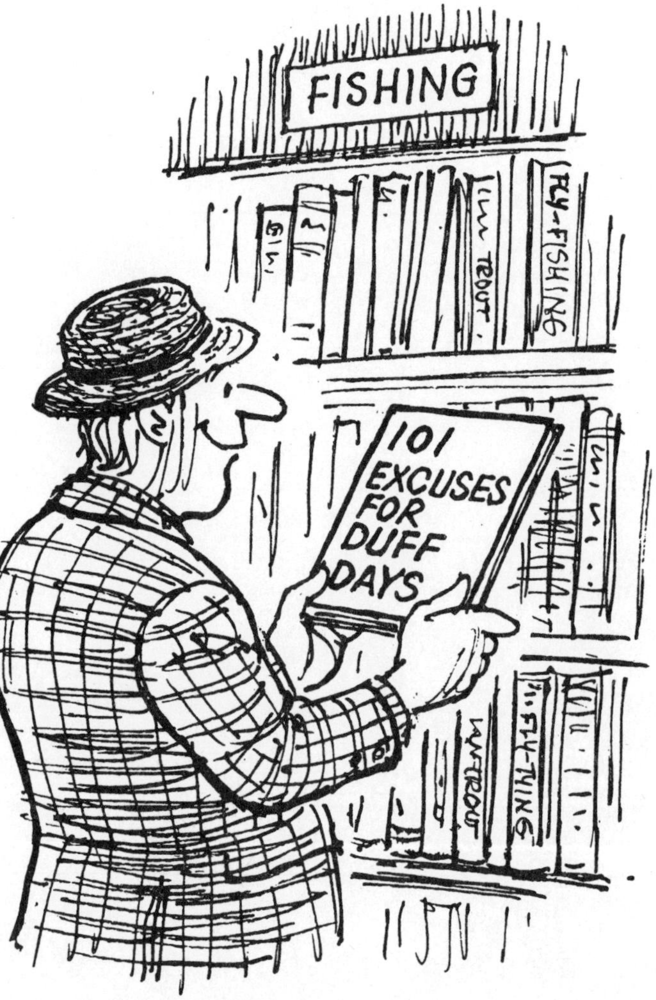
FISHING
FLY-FISHING
TROUT
101 EXCUSES FOR DUFF DAYS
FLY-TYING
TROUT

"And what pathetic excuse is on offer THIS time?"

'STRETCHING THE TRUTH' IS PERHAPS INEVITABLE.

"Serves you right for exaggerating so."

"I bet my dad's a bigger liar than your dad!"

EVERY WATER HAS A HOT-SPOT OR TWO.

"Hide it, quick — before everyone converges on your hot spot!"

'DUFFER'S FORTNIGHT', THE BRIEF APPEARANCE OF THE MAYFLY ON SOME WATERS, IS AN EVENT NOT TO BE MISSED.

"Grab your rods, gentlemen, there's a mayfly in my soup!"

IT'S A TIME WHEN THE MEREST TYRO MAY MAKE A GOOD BAG...

"Thanks for the loan of the mayfly, mister."

...A TIME WHEN DOCTORS' SICK-NOTES ARE EAGERLY SOUGHT AFTER.

"Tell you what, doctor, you give me a sick-note for another three days and I'll bring you a nice brace of rainbow trout."

FOR A FORTUNATE FEW THE END MAY COME WITH A SIGH OF RELIEF!

"Thank goodness we've seen the last of them for another year!"

A HATCH OF MIDGES ON THE WATER RAISES ONE'S EXPECTATIONS; A HATCH OF MIDGES ON THE BANK CAN RAISE ONE'S HACKLES!

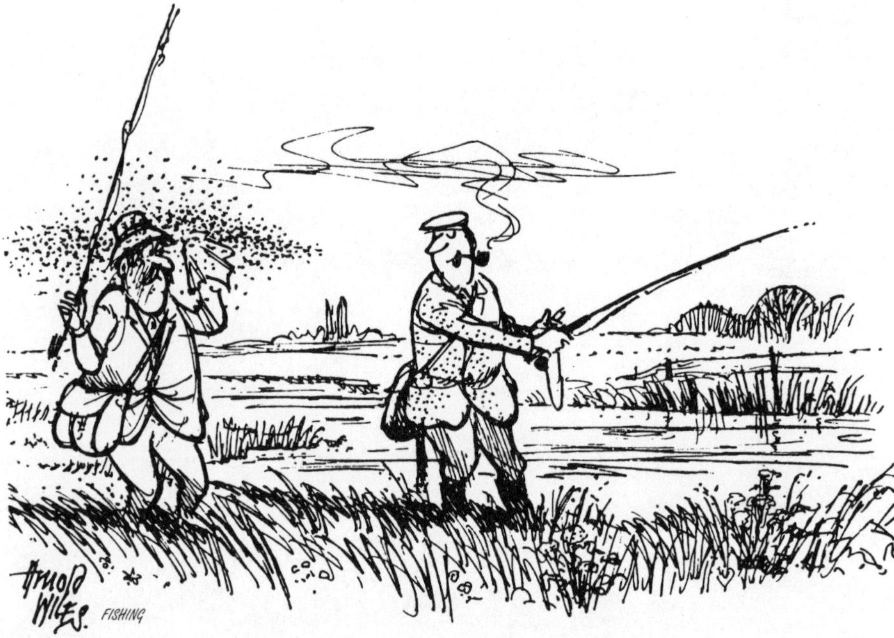
Arnold Wiles
FISHING

"It's called Flannigan's Old Special – best fly-repellent I've ever smoked!"

"This old hat I found in the attic is just the job!"

FOR MANY, EATING ONE'S TROUT IS A BONUS TO THE THRILL OF CATCHING THEM . . .

"Well, that's a laugh, dear — and I've an amusing little wine to go with it."

"That's not a tiny fish — that's an enormous frying-pan!"

FLY-FISHING & FLY-TYING

"They always order the trout but he prefers to catch them himself."

"For what we are about to receive, may we be truly thankful."

. . . BUT HAVING TO CATCH SOMETHING FOR THE POT CAN BE A DIFFERENT STORY!

"Go back and tell her Ladyship she can jolly well strike 'Truite meunière avec truffes suprême' off the menu tonight!"

WATERS HAVE TO BE STOCKED AND KEEPERED; POACHING CAN BE A PROBLEM AT TIMES.

"That notice means what it says, my lad!"

"Private water? That's the first I've heard of it."

"It's a tag with 'Private property — put me back!' printed on it."

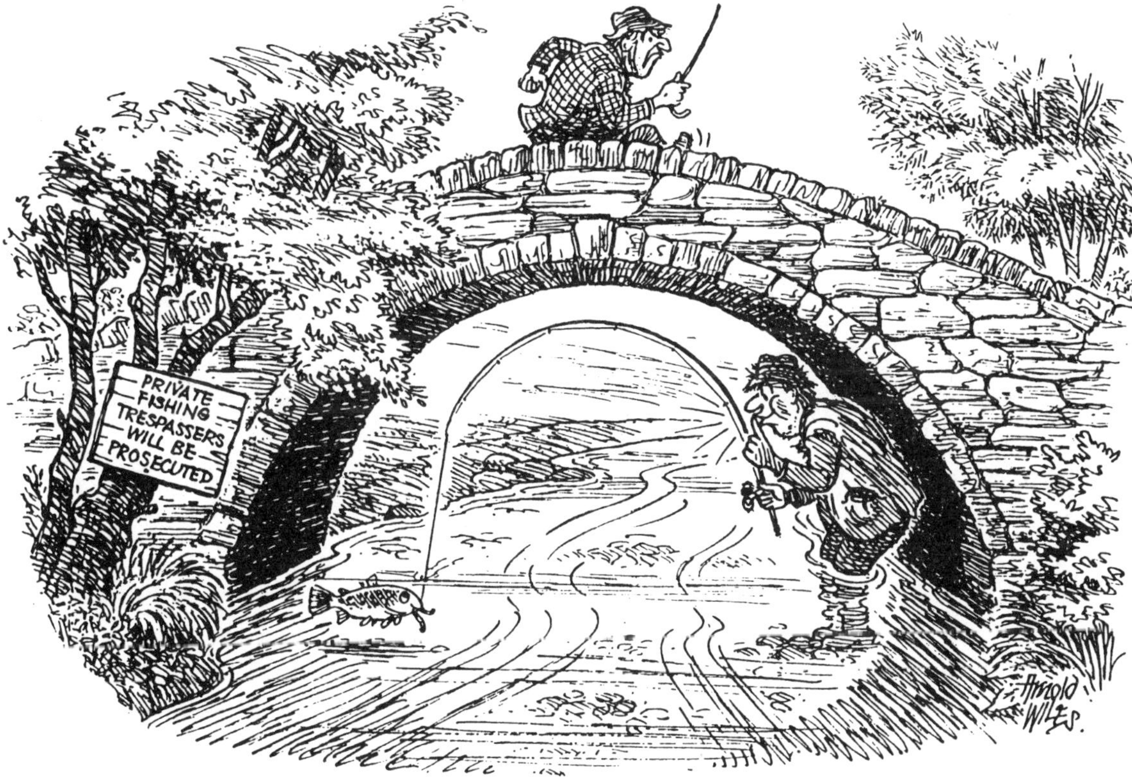
PRIVATE
FISHING
TRESPASSERS
WILL BE
PROSECUTED
Arnold
Wiles.

ANGLING PRESSURE CAN SOON MAKE WATERS FISHLESS WITHOUT REGULAR RESTOCKING.

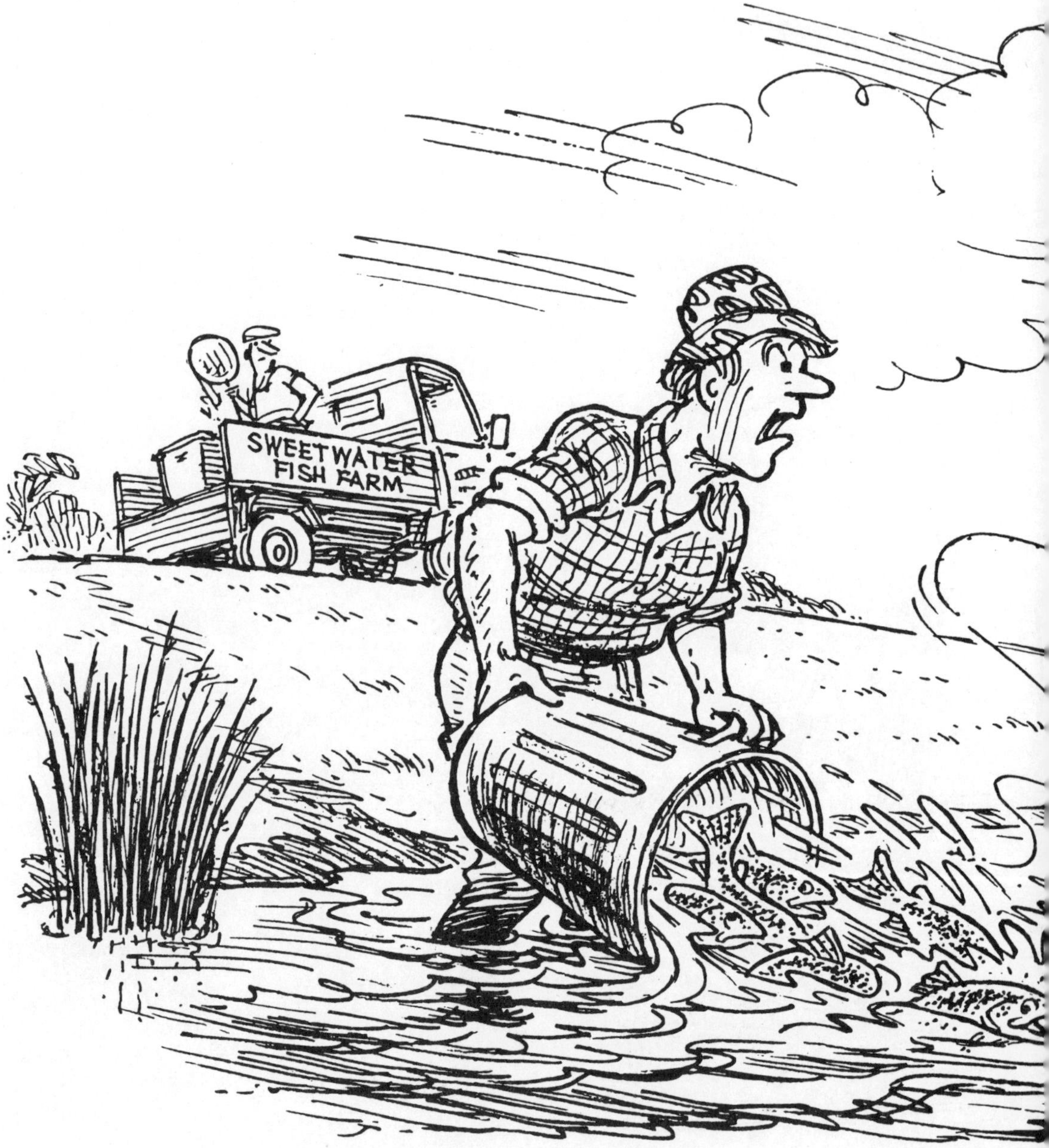
SWEETWATER FISH FARM

"Wait for it! Wait for it!"

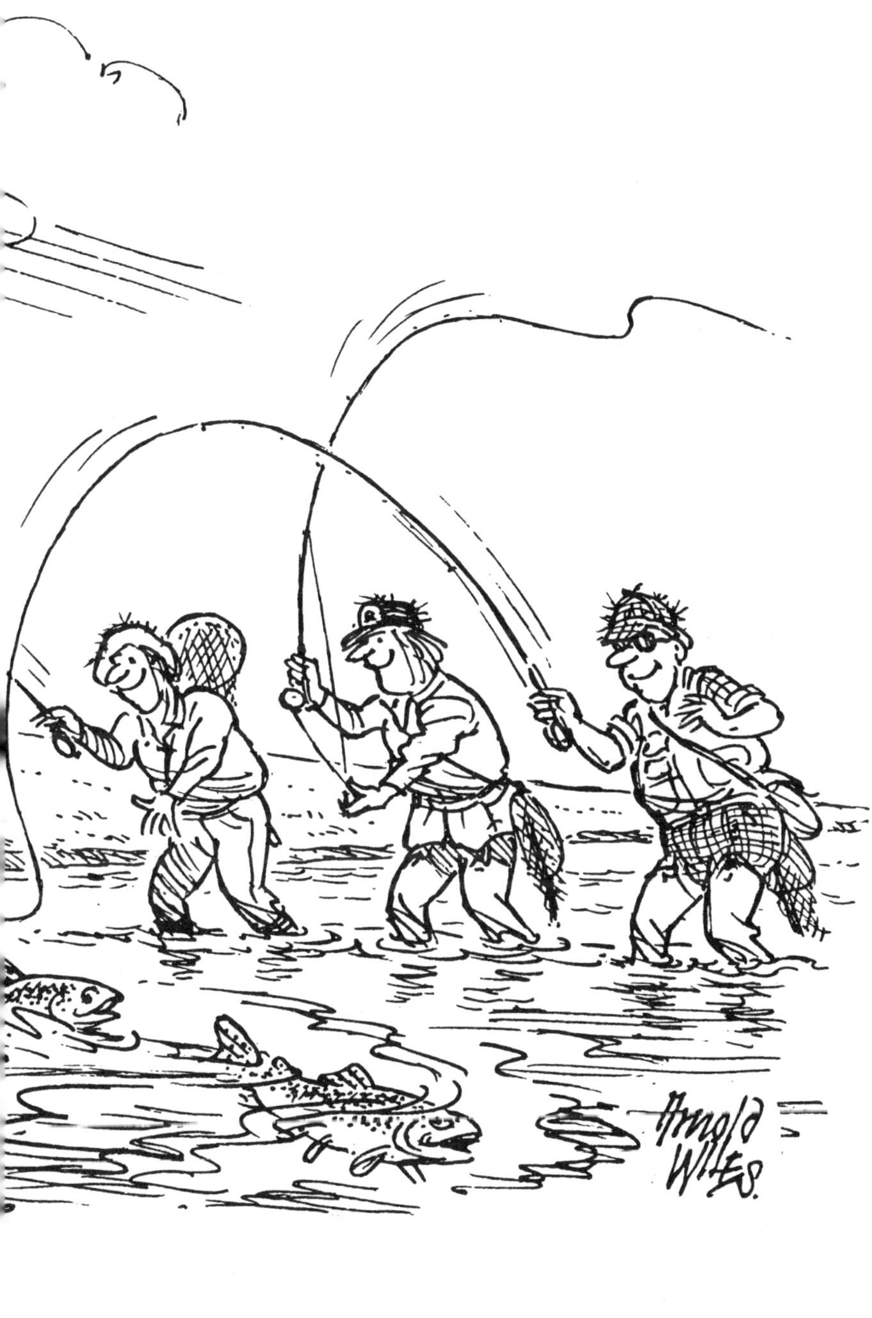
Arnold Wiles.

IN SOME AREAS, POLLUTION AND EXCESSIVE WATER ABSTRACTION MAY WELL LEAD TO THERE BEING NO RIVERS TO STOCK!

ANGLING TIMES

"So much for our day on the river — they've finally drunk it all!"

"Talk about water abstraction — this trout is developing legs!"

TROUT FLY-FISHING IS BIG BUSINESS, NOT ONLY IN THE TACKLE TRADE . . .

"A sight for sore eyes, if I may say so, sir — presumably you'll be wanting a fishing licence?"

"As long as he's drinking I suppose I shouldn't complain."

"Waiter, there's a fly in my soup!"

"We should have kept them apart. They own opposite banks on the best trout water!"

"No, mine's the one with the Sherry Spinner and the Tup's Indispensable."

"Only one fish between the lot of you — who caught it then?"

"No wonder he's a casting champion — he practises night and day!"

"I've a confession to make, Father, I tickled him out!"

'TACKLE-TINKERING' IS, OF COURSE, AN INTEGRAL PART OF THE SPORT.

"It's the same every season. He keeps his tackle in tip-top condition but allows himself to go to the dogs."

MANY FLY-FISHERS DREAM OF HAVING THEIR OWN LITTLE COTTAGE
BESIDE THEIR OWN TROUT-FILLED STREAM.

"I'll take it!"

"It looks suspiciously like a high-water mark to me."

IN RECENT YEARS TROUT FLY-FISHING HAS SEEN MANY
ADVANCES IN TACKLE AND TECHNIQUE. THE ADVENT OF
TUBE-FISHING MAY RAISE SOME EYEBROWS.

"Congratulations, dear! But I wish you'd take
your boat off before you come home."

BUT WHETHER YOU CAST THE FLY IN ENGLAND . . .

"I see that idiot in the pork pie hat has finally packed it in then."

...WALES...

"Why no, Mrs Jones, I haven't seen your husband all morning."

...SCOTLAND...

"When I caught a three-pounder here this morning there wasn't a soul in sight!"

...OR IRELAND – AND WHATEVER THE FUTURE MAY BRING...

"That's the third we've seen this morning. I reckon they're employed by the Irish Tourist Board."

. . . HERE'S WISHING TIGHT LINES TO ONE AND ALL!

"We let him clear out the coarse fish during the winter; I don't know how to tell him it's all over."